D1385438

Mary Queen of Scots

Five hundred years ago, Scotland and England were completely separate countries. In 1542, a Scottish princess was born. But her father, King James, wasn't happy. He had just lost a terrible battle against the English.

So many of my nobles are dead, I want to die too.

Soon King James died. His baby daughter, Mary, became queen.

Straight away the nobles started arguing about who should rule Scotland while Mary was growing up.

Your new Queen.

She's only six days old.

They also started planning Mary's marriage. Royal marriages were a good way of creating friendships between countries. The King of England wanted Mary to marry his son. So did the King of France.

I have a proposal from the King of France.

Scotland and England were old
enemies. Scotland and France were
old friends. So it was decided that
Mary should marry a French
prince when she was older.

6

Mary's mother and the nobles were worried that the English would be angry and kidnap Mary. So when Mary was five, she was sent to live in France.

Mary's husband-to-be was the French King's eldest son, François. He was timid, and often ill, but Mary liked him. When Mary was fifteen she and François got married.

The next year, François's father died. Now François and Mary were King and Queen of France, as well as of Scotland.

A year later, François died.
Mary was terribly upset. Back
in Scotland, Mary's mother
had died too.

Soon Mary decided that she should go and rule Scotland herself. The nobles who had been in charge weren't pleased. They liked having power.

The nobles thought Mary
followed the wrong religion, too.
At this time people were arguing
about the right way to worship
God. One group was called
Catholics, the other Protestants.

Mary was a Catholic. The nobles were mostly Protestants. They were worried Mary would try to turn Scotland back into a Catholic country.

But Mary didn't want to argue about religion. She knew it might start a war. So she said that Scotland could carry on being mostly Protestant, as long as she could still be Catholic.

You can keep your religion – as long as you let me keep mine.

Now Mary needed to marry again and have children so that everyone would know who would be next on the throne.

A young nobleman arrived from England, called Henry, Lord Darnley. Mary fell in love with him. She didn't realise that he was vain, spoilt and foolish.

The Scottish nobles hated him, but Mary took no notice. She and Darnley got married.

Soon Mary realised her mistake.

Mary and Darnley were expecting a baby, but they weren't getting on any more. Darnley was jealous of Mary's power. Mary's enemies realised this could be useful.

They decided to use Darnley
to attack Mary, and persuaded
him that he could rule alone.
Together they plotted to murder
several of Mary's supporters.

One night while Mary was having supper, Darnley and the plotters burst in. They grabbed one of her secretaries, whose name was David Riccio, and stabbed him to death.

The plotters probably hoped that the shock would make Mary lose her baby, and that she would die as well.

Mary was now a prisoner in her own palace. All night she tried to think of a way to escape.

In the morning, she pretended to be friendly to Darnley. Together they sneaked out of the palace to ride to another castle.

23

People flocked to support Mary. By the time she returned to Edinburgh the plotters had fled.

Three months later Mary gave birth to a baby boy called James. Then she heard rumours that Darnley was plotting to kidnap James and push her off the throne.

Mary decided she had to get rid of Darnley. The trouble was, a divorce might mean that James could not be the next king.

The nobles hated Darnley too. Some of them made a plan. Ever since, people have wondered whether Mary knew about this plan. She probably didn't, but no-one is sure.

Darnley was ill, and was staying at a house in Edinburgh. One night, the nobles – led by Bothwell and Balfour – sneaked into the house. They packed the cellar with gunpowder.

Later, in her palace, Mary was woken by a loud bang. Darnley's house had been blown up.

Darnley was found dead in the garden. But the blast hadn't killed him: he had been strangled.

Rumours started that Mary had planned the murder. To prove this wasn't true, she needed to catch the plotters. But Mary was frightened and ill. She relied on the nobles to advise her.

The nobles won't help investigate the murder. They did it!

The Queen is a murderess!

The noble Mary relied on most was Bothwell. People started saying that Mary and Bothwell had planned the murder together. The other nobles let Bothwell take the blame so that no one would suspect them.

I feel so ill. I need help.

Then Bothwell held a feast. He persuaded the other nobles to sign a paper saying he should marry Mary.

One day, when Mary was riding back to Edinburgh, Bothwell kidnapped her. Mary probably knew about the plan. But she didn't know that Bothwell would be violent with her and force her to marry him.

Mary was very upset, but knew she was too ill to rule alone.

Mary believed that the nobles wanted Bothwell as king. But by now many nobles hated Bothwell. They gathered an army. Mary and Bothwell gathered one too.

There was no battle, though. Mary agreed to go back to Edinburgh with the nobles if they let Bothwell escape.

Mary was taken to Edinburgh as a prisoner. Many people jeered, but some felt sorry for her. This worried the nobles.

They sent her away to an island in the middle of a lake called Loch Leven. Here they made Mary agree to give up the throne. Her baby son was declared King James VI. Mary never saw him again.

Almost a year later, Mary escaped from Loch Leven. She sailed to England, hoping that the English Queen, Elizabeth I, would help her.

Elizabeth wasn't sure what to do. She kept Mary locked up while she tried to decide. She didn't want to attack the Protestant nobles who were ruling Scotland, because she was Protestant too.

You are our guest.

Prisoner, you mean. Is this how you English treat a Queen?

Mary was Elizabeth's cousin. Many people thought Mary should be Queen of England if Elizabeth died. Some Catholics thought Mary should be Queen of England straight away.

As time went by, there were several plots to kill Elizabeth. It is difficult to tell how far Mary was involved with them.

At last, government spies said they had proof that Mary was plotting Elizabeth's death.

For years Elizabeth's ministers had been trying to persuade her to have Mary's head chopped off. Now Elizabeth agreed.

After nineteen years as a prisoner, Mary was executed. When Elizabeth heard the news she was grief-stricken and angry.

Further facts

James the Sixth and First

Elizabeth I never had any children. So, when she died, the English crown passed to the son of her cousin, Mary Queen of Scots. He was King James VI of Scotland already, and now he became James I of England too. Ever since then, the countries of the United Kingdom have shared the same monarch – and every one of them has been a descendant of Mary Queen of Scots.

The 'Casket Letters'

While Mary was a prisoner in England, some Scottish lords said they had found a casket, or box, of her letters. They said these letters proved Mary had planned Darnley's murder. The letters were shown to the English, but Mary was never allowed to see them.

Soon the letters disappeared altogether. Was it because they were forgeries – and the Scottish lords were afraid of being found out? This is a mystery people have puzzled over for more than four hundred years.

Some important dates in Mary Queen of Scot's lifetime

1542 Mary Stewart is born, the only surviving child of King James V of Scotland and his second wife, Mary of Guise.

6 days later James V dies and Mary becomes Queen of Scotland.

1548 Mary is sent to live in France.

1558 Mary marries the heir to the French throne, François, in Paris.

1559 King Henri II of France dies. François becomes King François II of France, and Mary becomes Queen.

1560 François dies, aged 16.

1561 Mary returns to Scotland.

1565 Mary marries Lord Darnley.

1566 Mary gives birth to a son, James.

1567 Darnley is murdered in Edinburgh.

1567 Mary marries the Earl of Bothwell.

1567 Mary is forced to give up the throne. Her son, aged 13 months, becomes King James VI.

1568 Mary escapes to England and is taken prisoner.

1587 Mary is executed at Fotheringay Castle.